\*GREATER Th  
 ALSO AVAI.  
  AUDIO.

# Greater Than a Tourist Book Series Reviews from Readers

I think the series is wonderful and beneficial for tourists to get information before visiting the city.

-Seckin Zumbul, Izmir Turkey

I am a world traveler who has read many trip guides but this one really made a difference for me. I would call it a heartfelt creation of a local guide expert instead of just a guide.

-Susy, Isla Holbox, Mexico

New to the area like me, this is a must have!

-Joe, Bloomington, USA

This is a good series that gets down to it when looking for things to do at your destination without having to read a novel for just a few ideas.

-Rachel, Monterey, USA

Good information to have to plan my trip to this destination.

-Pennie Farrell, Mexico

Great ideas for a port day.

-Mary Martin USA

Aptly titled, you won't just be a tourist after reading this book. You'll be greater than a tourist!

-Alan Warner, Grand Rapids, USA

Even though I only have three days to spend in San Miguel in an upcoming visit, I will use the author's suggestions to guide some of my time there. An easy read - with chapters named to guide me in directions I want to go.

-Robert Catapano, USA

Great insights from a local perspective! Useful information and a very good value!

-Sarah, USA

This series provides an in-depth experience through the eyes of a local. Reading these series will help you to travel the city in with confidence and it'll make your journey a unique one.

-Andrew Teoh, Ipoh, Malaysia

\>TOURIST

# GREATER THAN A TOURIST- WESTERN ALGARVE PORTUGAL

*50 Travel Tips from a Local*

Inês Tito

Greater Than a Tourist- Western Algarve Portugal Copyright © 2021 by CZYK Publishing LLC. All Rights Reserved.

All rights reserved. No part of this book may be reproduced in any form or by any electronic or mechanical means including information storage and retrieval systems, without permission in writing from the author. The only exception is by a reviewer, who may quote short excerpts in a review.
The statements in this book are of the authors and may not be the views of CZYK Publishing or Greater Than a Tourist.
First Edition
Cover designed by: Ivana Stamenkovic
Cover Image: https://pixabay.com/photos/portugal-algarve-ponta-da-piedade-4259398/
Image 1: By Philippe Salgarolo - Own work, CC BY-SA 4.0, https://commons.wikimedia.org/w/index.php?curid=72262772
Image 2: By Bengt Nyman - Own work, CC BY-SA 4.0, https://commons.wikimedia.org/w/index.php?curid=39230490
Image 3: By No machine-readable author provided. OsvaldoGago assumed (based on copyright claims). - No machine-readable source provided. Own work assumed (based on copyright claims)., CC BY-SA 3.0, https://commons.wikimedia.org/w/index.php?curid=810971
Image 4: By Photogal - Own work, CC BY-SA 3.0, https://commons.wikimedia.org/w/index.php?curid=4551898

CZYK Publishing Since 2011.
CZYKPublishing.com
Greater Than a Tourist
Lock Haven, PA
All rights reserved.
**ISBN:** 9798738721137

# >TOURIST

## 50 TRAVEL TIPS FROM A LOCAL

>TOURIST

# BOOK DESCRIPTION

With travel tips and culture in our guidebooks written by a local, it is never too late to visit Western Algarve. Greater Than a Tourist – Western Algarve, Portugal by Author Inês Tito offers the inside scoop on Europe's most beautiful secret. Most travel books tell you how to travel like a tourist. Although there is nothing wrong with that, as part of the 'Greater Than a Tourist' series, this book will give you candid travel tips from someone who has lived at your next travel destination. This guide book will not tell you exact addresses or store hours but instead gives you knowledge that you may not find in other smaller print travel books. Experience cultural, culinary delights, and attractions with the guidance of a Local. Slow down and get to know the people with this invaluable guide. By the time you finish this book, you will be eager and prepared to discover new activities at your next travel destination.

Inside this travel guide book you will find:

Visitor information from a Local
Tour ideas and inspiration
Save time with valuable guidebook information

Greater Than a Tourist- A Travel Guidebook with 50 Travel Tips from a Local. Slow down, stay in one place, and get to know the people and culture. By the time you finish this book, you will be eager and prepared to travel to your next destination.

vii

## OUR STORY

Traveling is a passion of the Greater than a Tourist book series creator. Lisa studied abroad in college, and for their honeymoon Lisa and her husband toured Europe. During her travels to Malta, an older man tried to give her some advice based on his own experience living on the island since he was a young boy. She was not sure if she should talk to the stranger but was interested in his advice. When traveling to some places she was wary to talk to locals because she was afraid that they weren't being genuine. Through her travels, Lisa learned how much locals had to share with tourists. Lisa created the Greater Than a Tourist book series to help connect people with locals. A topic that locals are very passionate about sharing.

>TOURIST

# TABLE OF CONTENTS

Book Description

Our Story

Table of Contents

Dedication

About the Author

How to Use This Book

From the Publisher

WELCOME TO > TOURIST

1. The Locals

2. Getting Around

3. Highway Or National Road?

4. Hiring Transportation

5. The Crowds

6. Fresh Fish Days

7. Learning A Bit Of Portuguese

8. Get Those Legs Moving

9. Suestada

10. Bottoms Up!

11. Where Do We Go Now?

12. The Costa Vicentina

13. The End Of The World

14. Get Your Surfboard Ready!

15. Barnacles?

16. The Pearl of The West Coast

17. Sweet Potatoes
18. A Beach Cove And A Needle's Rock
19. The Land Of The Adventurous
20. Can you hold your breath?
21. The Home Of The Portuguese Discoveries
22. Ponta da Piedade
23. Plenty Of Fish… In Your Plate
24. Fado
25. Midnight Bathing
26. "Portus Magnus"
27. The Old Town
28. The Riverside
29. Something Old, Something New
30. Alcalar
31. Ocean Revival
32. Beaches
33. I Feel The Need, The Need For Speed!
34. The Ancient Capital
35. When A Museum Becomes The Artifact
36. Get On The Time Machine
37. Going Up The River
38. Monchique
39. The Mountain Top
40. The Rarest Water In Portugal
41. Hmmm… yummy!
42. The "Medronho" Spirit

>TOURIST

43. Lagoa
44. The River Mills
45. A Hermitage On The Cliffs
46. A Fishermen's Village
47. The Western Algarve Wonders
48. Home Is Where Your Hearth Is
49. The "Azulejos"
50. Discovering Ferragudo
TOP REASONS TO BOOK THIS TRIP
Packing and Planning Tips
Travel Questions
Travel Bucket List
NOTES

>TOURIST

# DEDICATION

This book is dedicated to Pedro for his support on all my insane ideas.

>TOURIST

# ABOUT THE AUTHOR

Inês is a Portuguese writer, self-taught photographer and nature lover born in Ferragudo and living in Monchique. She also lived in Évora for five years during her studies in Work and Organizational Psychology. She loves hiking, feeling the crispy breeze from the ocean and the smell of a wet forest after heavy rain. She loves to travel and get immersed in other cultures, but the Algarve will forever be her home.

>TOURIST

# HOW TO USE THIS BOOK

The *Greater Than a Tourist* book series was written by someone who has lived in an area for over three months. The goal of this book is to help travelers either dream or experience different locations by providing opinions from a local. The author has made suggestions based on their own experiences. Please check before traveling to the area in case the suggested places are unavailable.

**Travel Advisories**: As a first step in planning any trip abroad, check the Travel Advisories for your intended destination.
https://travel.state.gov/content/travel/en/traveladvisories/traveladvisories.html

## FROM THE PUBLISHER

Traveling can be one of the most important parts of a person's life. The anticipation and memories that you have are some of the best. As a publisher of the Greater Than a Tourist, as well as the popular *50 Things to Know* book series, we strive to help you learn about new places, spark your imagination, and inspire you. Wherever you are and whatever you do I wish you safe, fun, and inspiring travel.

Lisa Rusczyk Ed. D.
CZYK Publishing

>TOURIST

# WELCOME TO
# > TOURIST

>TOURIST

*Algarve's typical coast (Marinha Beach, near Lagoa)*

*Partial view of Carvoeiro*

*The bog fountain in Alte*

*Beach in Quarteira*

# >TOURIST

*Better to see something once
than hear about it a thousand times*

– Asian Proverb

Algarve is a rich and diverse region located in the south of Portugal. With an area of almost 5.000 square kilometers, it is limited by the Monchique-Caldeirão mountain range on the northside, by the Guadiana river on the east, and by the Atlantic Ocean on the south and west sides.

Since the 8th century BC, humans have occupied this strip of land between the mountains and the Atlantic Ocean. Archeologists have found evidence of many different tribes and civilizations that have left their marks on our lives up to this day.

The first inhabitants were the Conni, a group of tribes of Celtic origin that developed written language and established contact with the Phoenician civilization by exchanging the local products.

The Conii, after many years of wars with the Lusitanian, Celtic and other Iberian tribes, surrendered to the Romans. Having the territory under their control, the Romans explored what the land and sea had to offer and the Algarve met a prosperous era of economic and cultural development. Due to its location, the region was an important fluvial route for commerce in the Guadiana and Arade rivers and a must-stop point in the maritime routes between the roman ports in the Mediterranean Sea, Gaul and Britain.

The Roman rule met its end with the early 5th century AD when the Visigoths, along with the Suevi and other smaller Germanic tribes invaded the Iberian Peninsula. When in 585 the Suevi kingdom was overthrown, the Visigoths took over and adopted Christianism as the official religion. Scholars and archeologists have found many artifacts left behind by the Visigoths such as ceramic pots and pans in Silves, a chapiter in Porches and a necropolis in Lagos.

By the time the Moorish arrived in the Algarve, they began the longest occupation of the territory, which lasted for 800 years. In the 8th century AD, the Jewish people were weary of persecutions from the Visigoth king and from the Catholic church itself. Therefore, a group of powerful Jews, that controlled the Gibraltar passage, decided to help the Islamic and Berber army to enter the Iberian Peninsula and put an end to years of religious intolerance. As such, in the year 711, the first Moorish army invaded the Algarve. The integration of local traditions and religious

>TOURIST

freedom were two of the decisive elements that led to the success of the Moorish rule.

Silves became the most important city due to its location: the land's natural geography protected the city and its castle from any foreign attacks and the Arade river allowed quick access to the Atlantic Ocean. Nowadays, the Islamic heritage can be found all throughout the Algarve in architecture, gastronomy and even in many Portuguese words.

The "Reconquista" (literally translates to "Reconquer") refers to the historic period when the Christian kings in the Iberian Peninsula intended to dominate the territory and expel the Umayyad Caliphate. Although the Portuguese kingdom was founded in 1143, the Algarve was the last territory to be conquered, mainly because the mountain range worked as a natural frontier between the northern lands and the Algarve. In the second attempt to consolidate the Portuguese presence in the territory, king D. Afonso III, in 1249, finally conquered the last Moorish-occupied cities of Faro, Albufeira, Porches and Silves.

The Portuguese king recognized the influence of the Moorish in the territory and reconstructed the infrastructures left behind, using them for the good of the kingdom.

The western Algarve, known as the "Barlavento", became of great importance during the 15<sup>th</sup> century when the Portuguese set sail to discover the New World. The small hamlet of Sagres was the chosen location for the departure of the "caravelas" (caravels). The Infante D. Henrique, the fifth son of king D. João I, was the pioneer of Portuguese maritime exploration, by conquering Ceuta and occupying the Atlantic island of Azores and Madeira. During his lifetime and under his command, the Portuguese caravels traveled along the African coast to the islands known today as Cape Verde, in 1455. The Infante D. Henrique made Lagos his home and his name became connected to the city's history.

Over the next 300 years, the Portuguese armada grew larger and reached new lands from the eastern coast of Africa, India, China, Japan, Australia, Vanuatu, Newfoundland and Brazil. During this period, Sagres maintained its reputation as one of the preferred places for departure, only followed by Lisbon.

The 18<sup>th</sup> century marked the decline of the Portuguese influence in its colonies and the rise of new powerful competitors, such as the English, the French and the Netherlander, for new maritime routes. The great earthquake of 1755, which vanished

>TOURIST

most of the country, led the Algarve through a cycle towards decay.

The prosperity once known during the Moorish occupation and the "Descobertas" (Portuguese maritime travels) ceased to exist. The locals felt left behind and the following centuries were marked by many rebellions.

In the 20th century, the Algarve was a rural and forgotten region of the country, with an economy based on the traditional agriculture, fishing and canned fish industry. A tremendous shift happened in the 1960s when tourism activities grew exponentially. The newer generations were presented with employment opportunities they never knew before, which led them closer to the Algarve's coastline where beach tourism grew. Due to this change in the local economy, the region became one of the country's hotspots for beach vacation and the countryside met the first signs of a rural exodus.

Currently, the Algarve is well-known for its sunny weather and golden sand beaches and has established itself as one of the preferred beach destinations in Portugal and Europe. However, there is much more to discover. From the coastline to foggy mountains, this book will show you the best places and experiences.

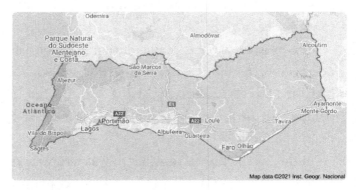

**Faro District**
Portugal

>TOURIST

## Lagos
## Western Algarve
## Portugal
## Climate

|  | High | Low |
|---|---|---|
| January | 61 | 47 |
| February | 61 | 47 |
| March | 64 | 51 |
| April | 66 | 53 |
| May | 71 | 57 |
| June | 75 | 61 |
| July | 77 | 63 |
| August | 78 | 64 |
| September | 77 | 63 |
| October | 73 | 59 |
| November | 66 | 52 |
| December | 62 | 49 |

### GreaterThanaTourist.com

Temperatures are in Fahrenheit degrees.
Source: NOAA

>TOURIST

# 1. THE LOCALS

As a local, born and raised in the Algarve, I will always say this is the most beautiful part of the country. I simply love the place that shaped who I am and to where I always return to. This is my home!

If you ask me why I like this land so much, I will tell you so much and even so, I will leave out most of it.

While you are visiting, you will see how the Algarvians are proud of the land's natural beauty and its uniqueness. We are the product of different civilizations, creeds, beliefs and traditions and hold centuries' worth of knowledge that cannot be found anywhere else in the country.

For all these reasons, and much more, the Algarvians wish that you enjoy this land as much as they do!

# 2. GETTING AROUND

Traveling to the Algarve is quite simple. There are plenty of options, depending on where you are coming from. The most used and easily accessible is the Faro Airport since it can connect you with the main European airports and with Lisbon, in case you are traveling from outside Europe. Once your plane lands, you can get on a shuttle or private transfer, a taxi, an Uber, or hire a rental car. The train and bus stations are located in Faro city center (about a ten-minute drive), meaning that you would still need to get a taxi or an Uber. In any case, the fastest way to get to your destination would be the private transfer or Uber driver.

# 3. HIGHWAY OR NATIONAL ROAD?

If you enjoy driving, even if it's outside of your comfort zone, hire a car and use the highway A22 or the national road 125. These are the quickest options to get around in the Algarve, especially if you want to travel for more than 20 kilometers.

National road 125 is the oldest route connecting the Algarve from one end to the other and it is the main option for the locals to drive around since it connects many small villages and cities. For this reason, road maintenance is made quite often. You

>TOURIST

may find heavy traffic when arriving in the larger cities of Olhão, Faro, Albufeira, Portimão or Lagos, especially on weekdays.

The highway A22 has a toll system that, sometimes, can be a bit tricky. Since there aren't any paying tolls along the road, this means that the car's license plate you are using will be photographed and the invoice will be sent to the address where the car is registered. Unfortunately, this only works on Portuguese license plates. Do not fear, however! This can be easily solved! There is a website named Portugal Tolls where you can buy a prepaid card that will be associated with the car's license plate so that you can get around and not worry about the incoming bill. Also, most rental car companies prepare all their vehicles to make sure there aren't any "surprise" fees at the end of your vacation.

# 4. HIRING TRANSPORTATION

Over the years, the population living in the Algarve and the number of visitors increased, which required the local authorities to update and invest in the public transportation system. Companies such as EVA or Frota Azul provide transportation between cities and villages throughout the region. All the timetables available can be seen on their websites.

However, in the main cities, you can find small buses that circulate all over town, usually every 20 or 30 minutes. Since each municipality is responsible for this service, you will need to check the timetables on each website. In the Western Algarve you can use the company "Onda Azul" in Lagos and the company "Vai e Vem" in Portimão.

Also, some of the bus stop names were given considering what the locals used to name those places and, sometimes, they are not exactly the same as described on the city's maps. In case you feel lost, ask for help at the ticket shop or even to the bus driver. They will help you get to your destination.

## 5. THE CROWDS

The warm and sunny weather transformed the Algarve into a beach hotspot during the Summer. July and August are the busiest months since both locals and tourists enjoy most of their vacation time at the beach. Especially on weekends, you may find larger crowds.

>TOURIST

In 2020, the Portuguese Agency for the Environment developed an app called "InfoPraia" which has updated information on all the beaches, including the sea conditions, air temperature, wind speed and, most important, if the beach is at maximum capacity. This allows you to organize your beach trip in advance and avoid the crowds.

Although the name is in Portuguese, you can download it and select the menu in English.

During the Summer, if you are planning on going to the supermarket or the local fresh fish and vegetable market, my advice is to get there earlier in the morning. You will have more variety and the freshest products available. Also, the sooner you get there, the fewer people you will find.

Are you looking forward to enjoying the Algarve in a less crowded time of the year? If that is the case, I advise you to plan your vacation for May, June, September and the first half of October. The good weather will allow you to enjoy the beach and all other natural landscapes, but with fewer tourists.

Over the Winter, which is considered low season for beach tourism, the golf courses are filled with amateur and professional golfers who enjoy the amene temperatures of the Algarve.

25

# 6. FRESH FISH DAYS

Looking for a taste of the freshest fish on the coast? You have come to the right place!

The Algarve submarine geography is characterized by a plateau, meaning the bottom of the ocean has the perfect depth to accommodate a larger variety of fish, mollusk and shellfish. Sardines and horse mackerel are the most common species and the preferred both by locals and visitors.

The fishing boats arrive from the sea early in the morning, sometimes even before sunrise. The fish is quickly traded with the local restaurants and markets, to get in its best condition to the final customer. As such, if you are craving grilled sardines have them at lunch, so they are the freshest.

The fresh fish market is a great way to see all the species available on our coastline. Since the local fishermen take Sunday and Monday as their days off, the best days to visit the market are from Tuesday to Saturday. The fish you find on Sundays and Mondays usually come from fish farms. Although they are high quality, the taste is not the same.

>TOURIST

# 7. LEARNING A BIT OF PORTUGUESE

If your native language is not of Latin origin, you may find Portuguese extra difficult to learn. The nasal sounds and the prominent "r's" make it hard for an English-speaking person to speak Portuguese with the right accent.

When you are in Portugal, you may hear the word "obrigado" (thank you) in different contexts which might be confusing. The word derives from the verb "obrigar" (meaning to force something or someone), but can also be used as an adjective when you want to say "thank you". According to the Portuguese grammar, the gentlemen must say "obrigado" (phonetically is o.bɾi.'ga.du) and the ladies must say "obrigada" (phonetically is o.bɾi.'ga.dɐ). I'll put your mind at ease…this is a common doubt, even for the Portuguese native speakers, so you have nothing to worry about!

To make this even harder, the Algarvians have an accent that cannot be found anywhere else in the country. We have the bad habit of cutting off the last vowel, especially if it finishes with an "o", and replace it with an "e". As such, you will often hear the locals say "obrigade" (phonetically is o.bɾi.ˈga.dɨ).

For this reason, while you are visiting the Algarve and you say "obrigado", we do appreciate your effort. And in case you don't get it right at first, don't worry, we will help you get the accent right (the Algarvian one)!

# 8. GET THOSE LEGS MOVING

As a local, I have found the most beautiful landscapes through hiking. I have learned about places I have never heard of, some of them not even the elderly have ever known.

Fortunately, the website Visit Algarve, promoted by the region's tourism authorities, developed a hiking guide with trails all over the Algarve.

There is a route named "Via Algarviana" that extends for 300 kilometers between Cape St. Vincent and Alcoutim and it is the longest in the Algarve. This route is divided into sections and there are other smaller routes, in case you wish to hike or walk in a shorter area.

>TOURIST

The existing guides, both from Via Algarviana or Visit Algarve, describe the standard signaling used to identify the trails on the field, as well as its GPS coordinates, description of the flora and fauna, level of difficulty, altitude variations and, of course, a map. If you enjoy birdwatching or photography, any trail you choose will be a great opportunity for both.

Over the years, I have found some favorites. I hope you enjoy them as much as I do:

"Ao Sabor da Maré" – the river estuary of Alvor is surrounded by dunes. This five-kilometer trail is made on a wooden promenade and dirt road. Since it is easily accessible, most of it can be done even if you have a walking disability.

"Caminho dos Promontórios" – this trail will take you on a journey through the cliffs between the villages of Ferragudo and Carvoeiro. It is a seven-kilometer route where you can find some of the most secret beaches along the coast, many of them only accessible by boat.

"Rota das Cascatas" – located in the Monchique mountain, through this 20-kilometer route, you will have the opportunity to see some of the largest waterfalls in the western Algarve. Due to the influence of the Mediterranean in the region's climate, it is recommended to do this trail during

Spring. There will be plenty of water falling and the weather will also be warmer than in the Winter. If you choose the Summer or Autumn, it is most likely that the waterfalls are dry.

# 9. SUESTADA

This is what we say when the Algarve is affected by the southeast winds coming from North Africa. The sky is filled with the Sahara Desert sand particles and it acquires a golden glare. The air temperature rises, the humidity lowers and wind gusts become stronger. The best part about the "Suestada" is the sea temperature. The waters are also warmer, sometimes rising to 27 Celsius degrees.

For you to enjoy this weather, find a beach facing west. The cliffs will protect you from the wind gusts.

During the "Suestada", the ocean currents also change, becoming increasingly stronger with higher waves. While you stay in the Algarve check the sea conditions before you go to the beach or anywhere close to the shore. Also, the local authorities suggest that you choose life-guarded beaches and swim parallel to the shoreline.

>TOURIST

# 10. BOTTOMS UP!

As a tourist in Portugal, when you request a good Portuguese wine, the sommelier will certainly recommend you a bottle from Alentejo or Douro, since these are the most renowned and prized wines in the country.

However, since you are visiting the western Algarve, you will have to try a glass of local wine. The warm temperatures in the Summer and amene Winter climate gather some of the best conditions for the vineyard's good development. For this reason, in the last 30 years, the wine industry in the Algarve has grown quickly.

The red Algarvian wines stand out from others in other regions of the country due to their fruity taste and fresh feel. On the other hand, the white and rosé wines are much lighter and easily drinkable.

The wineries are eager to welcome you and show you their best work. So, why not book a guided tour and have a wine tasting?

At "Quinta dos Vales", in Estômbar, it is possible to enjoy a private wine tasting tour and visit the winery. Through the gardens and vineyards, you can observe contemporary art, designed and made on site.

In the surroundings of Silves, there are the award-winning wineries of "Quinta do Francês" and "Cabrita Wines". The "Quinta do Francês" is a recent project that started in the early 2000s and quickly became one of the big names in the industry. The "Cabrita Wines" is a forty-year-old family business that elevates the local grapes, originally used by Mr. Cabrita Senior. Wine tastings and vineyard tours are available at both locations.

# 11. WHERE DO WE GO NOW?

Maybe Gun's n' Roses were inspired by the Algarve when they wrote Sweet Child of Mine, but who knows? I'll ask Slash or Axel Rose the next time I see them!

You may feel lost with all the information, places and activities you will find in the Algarve. Well, consider what you enjoy the most... Is it hiking, bird watching or sailing? Are you more of a history fan and enjoy visiting architectural landmarks, museums, castles and fortresses? Or do you prefer the

>TOURIST

contemporary feel of the biggest cities? The options are endless!

# 12. THE COSTA VICENTINA

The landscape here changes abruptly. Where the land meets the ocean to the west, the highest and darkest cliffs of the Algarve stand against the heavy waves. Closer to Alentejo, never-ending sandy beaches contrast with dark cliffs.

# 13. THE END OF THE WORLD

The Cape St. Vicent, located in the Costa Vicentina Natural Park, is the most southwestern point in Europe. The Romans used to call it "Promontorium Sacrum" (Sacred Promontory), as a tribute to the god Saturn. The locals believed that nothing else existed after that mass of land invaded the ocean and for this reason named it "The End of World". However, with the discovery of new lands across the ocean, the cape received the name, St. Vincent, as a homage to the Christian martyr who, according to a local legend, died at the cape and was later on taken back to Lisbon by boat and followed by two crows which are now part of the city's coat of arms.

The existing lighthouse was built in 1846, over a Franciscan convent. Over the years, the building has been updated and amplified. Nowadays, it keeps its reputation as an important landmark for maritime routes and it hosts the Lighthouse Museum.

The cape is also a reference point to migratory birds, on their way to northern Africa, and to marine mammals, which can be observed according to their migratory patterns.

You can visit this natural landmark all by yourself or, if you prefer, get a guided tour so that you can learn more about the natural wonders this place has to show you. In any case, please wear a warm sweater! Even on the hottest summer days, the cape is one of the windiest and coldest places you can find in the Algarve, with the temperature dropping an astonishing ten Celsius degrees between morning and evening.

>TOURIST

# 14. GET YOUR SURFBOARD READY!

The Costa Vicentina coastline is the number one hotspot for surf in the Algarve. Travelers from around the world enjoy the waves available any time of the year. Amongst the most well-known surfers are Robert Trujillo, Metallica's bass player, or the big wave surfer Garreth McNamara. Both of them have shown the world how beautiful these beaches are.

Although I could name all the beaches, I'll give you three names that are some of my favorites: Praia do Amado, Praia da Arrifana and Praia dos Montes Clérigos. You can thank me later!

Grab your surfboard and try it for yourself! Don't have one? Not a problem! There are plenty of surf schools in the cities of Portimão and Lagos, but you can also find them on site. Most of these schools provide lessons for any level of surfers. However, if you are an experienced surfer, you can rent all the equipment you need and choose the beach you fancy the most.

# 15. BARNACLES?

Not any kind of barnacles… goose barnacles to be precise! In Portuguese, they are called "percebes", which many times is literally translated to "understands" (the Portuguese are very funny, don't you think?).

This shellfish enjoys the colder and fury waters of the Costa Vicentina shores. The biggest of their kind grow in the most inaccessible cliffs and the shellfish gatherers risk their lives to catch them, by climbing the cliffs to collect the barnacles by hand.

During December and January, it is not allowed, by law, to catch goose barnacles. This restriction aims to maintain the sustainability of natural resources.

The goose barnacles are boiled in seawater and seasoned with a tiny pinch of salt. As soon as the water starts to boil, this delicacy is ready! The shell and its insides are not eatable. However, once you rip the gooseneck there is a rosy flesh. Go on… taste it! You will feel like you have the ocean in your mouth. It's something out of this world!

Next time you see "understands" written on a restaurant menu, go inside and ask for "percebes"!

>TOURIST

# 16. THE PEARL OF THE WEST COAST

Aljezur is located deep in the Costa Vicentina Natural Park.

The first settlements were Neolithic tribes who were established here. However, it was only in the 10th century when the Moorish arrived that the village was founded. The Castle of Aljezur, which can be visited nowadays, was built by the Moorish on top of the highest hill, to protect the village and its surroundings.

The name Aljezur has its origins in the Arabic word "al jazair", the island in English. Just as it happened with other places in the Algarve, the village was conquered by the Portuguese in the 13th century.

The village was also an important reference during the II World War. Although Portugal remained neutral, due to its strategic location, the German and English navy boats often made way through Portuguese waters and the skies were filled with their aircraft. The Battle of Aljezur, as it became known, was the stage of air combat between the Nazis and the Allied Forces, for almost one hour. In the end, a German plane crashed and seven Nazi soldiers died.

At the time, Portugal was under the dictatorship of António Salazar and, for this reason, the news about this event were never published. Nevertheless, the locals took care of the soldier's bodies and buried them regardless of their beliefs. Even today, their graves are often visited by Germans living in the area.

# 17. SWEET POTATOES

In recent years, the Sweet Potato of Aljezur has increased its popularity. Once a year, the village holds a festival between November and December, where the local producers showcase the best the land has to offer.

What distinguishes this Sweet Potato from any other are the soil and weather conditions where it grows. The sandy soil in this part of the western Algarve allows the tuber to grow freely without any obstacles. The sunny weather for most of the time and the low humidity leads to a sweeter end product. Since the sweet potato in Aljezur has a specific trademark, most of the production is biological, meaning that no chemicals are used.

>TOURIST

The festival also presents local chefs that show the visitors endless cooking possibilities. In the end, you can buy a few as a souvenir. If you have the chance, try out the octopus "cataplana" with sweet potato. It is to die for!

# 18. A BEACH COVE AND A NEEDLE'S ROCK

The fishermen's village of Arrifana stands on top of shell-shaped dark cliffs. On the north side, you can visit the ruins of the village's fortress, built in the Middle Ages to protect the population from the Moroccans who invaded its shores and kidnapped the locals to be sold as slaves in Argel.

The strategic location of the fortress provides a breath-taking view of the village and its beach. Close by, down a steep hill, there's the Portinho da Arrifana, a small port used by the local fishermen to keep the boats and released them into the ocean, as well as keeping their work tools protected from the elements.

Every year, on the last weekend of July, the fishermen get together for the "Festa dos Pescadores" (Fishermen's Feast), where the local priest joins a boat procession and blesses the fishing boats at Pedra da Agulha, a stand-alone rock close to the black cliffs. As soon as they return to the port, the grills, fish and beer are ready to welcome everyone. For a small amount, you can buy the entrance ticket and join the festivities, not worrying about any extra fees. The amount gathered is given to the local fisherman's association. You will also get a one-of-a-kind beer mug made by local artisans. Every year there is a new design to celebrate another year of feasting. With the mug in your hand, you are now ready to eat grilled sardines and drink as much beer as you would like. Through the night, local artists entertain the crowd.

Since the feast has a very low-key vibe, you don't have to worry about dress codes. From my personal experience, wear comfortable beachwear and take a warm sweater. Since you are closer to the ocean, the evenings are colder than on land. When you leave the feast, you will likely smell grilled sardines all over, so I would advise you not to wear your nicest clothes.

>TOURIST

# 19. THE LAND OF THE ADVENTUROUS

In Portugal, you will find two kinds of Sagres: the beer and the village. For the time being, I'll let you know about the last.

The village of Sagres is part of the Vila do Bispo municipality and it is located east of the Cape St. Vicent. Due to its importance during the 15th century, Infante D. Henrique founded a nautical school named "Escola de Sagres", intending to educate new generations of sailors with the knowledge of cartography, astronomy and geography.

The Sagres Fortress was built also during the 15th century and it is one of the most visited monuments in the Algarve. Since it was restored many times throughout history, it is possible to see different architectural styles ranging from the Renaissance to the Neoclassic. Considering the amount of information on this monument, I recommend you to do a guided tour. This way you will not miss any detail.

# 20. CAN YOU HOLD YOUR BREATH?

To be honest, you don't really have to for the next tip.

Another great way of getting to know Sagres history and its importance is through scuba diving. The company "Pura Vida Dive House" offers a large variety of experiences where you will have the opportunity to visit underwater caves, coral riffs and shipwrecks from the I World War. Whether you are a beginner or an experienced diver, looking to expand your diving skills, there are freediving and open water diving courses available.

# 21. THE HOME OF THE PORTUGUESE DISCOVERIES

Lagos, once known by the Romans as "Lacóbriga", was later occupied by the Visigoths and the Moorish and later claimed by the Christians in the 12th century. However, the city's name entered the history books in the 15th century with the "Descobertas". The golden age of maritime trading

>TOURIST

and commerce and the innovations developed by the Portuguese transformed Lagos into one of the richest cities in the country. At the time, this was the place to go if you wanted to sail around the world. Nowadays, in Lagos, you can visit the City's Walls, the Wax Museum of the Portuguese Discoveries and the Governor's Castle.

# 22. PONTA DA PIEDADE

At a short distance from Lagos city center (only three kilometers away), lies a rock formation by the sea called "Ponta da Piedade". The cliffs are dated between 20 to 7 million years old and were defined by sea and wind erosion. Paleontologists have found coral fossils, evidence of extinct fishes and even teeth of giant sharks.

During the 18th and 19th centuries, Ponta da Piedade acted as a guard post, warning of incoming ships that might attack the city. The lighthouse was built in 1912 over the ruins of a hermitage and it is still in use today, being seen as far as Portimão (20 kilometers away).

There are a few options when visiting this promontory: you can walk or bike from Lagos city center, rent a car, hire a taxi or an uber or get on a guided tour by boat. Whatever option you choose, you can always observe the cliffs from land or sea.

My advice: go on a guided kayak tour! There are a few companies in Lagos providing this experience and it is the best way to visit the Ponta da Piedade caves. The kayaks departure from Ponta da Bandeira Fortress (in Lagos) and the local guide will give a short briefing on safety procedures and the itinerary. If there is a larger group, probably you will have more than one guide. The best part is that they understand not everyone is as fit as they think they are, so they let you take your time and make a few stops along the way to regroup. Once you reach the caves, even if the tide is high, the guide will show all the names and curious facts. You might be lucky enough to enter some caves that boats cannot access. Also, they will provide a waterproof bag that you can use for your belongings. However, the lighter you go into the kayak the better. Since you are at sea, and sometimes it gets windy and you might get some splashes, so I suggest that you wear your bikini or bathing suit. And, of course, don't forget to wear sunscreen.

Probably, you will have sore arms the next morning, but this is definitely a worthy experience.

>TOURIST

# 23. PLENTY OF FISH... IN YOUR PLATE

After all the effort of paddling under the sun and of getting splashed with seawater, you have earned your right to a meal worthy of kings!

In the earth of Lagos, lies the smallest restaurant, hidden in an alley, named the "Escondidinho". Although there are a few meat options, the specialty is the freshest fish of the day. You can order a plate of grilled sardines or, if you are adventurous enough, you can order the all-you-can-eat menu. They will only stop sending grilled fish to your table when you beg them to stop!

Since the place is quite small, and to avoid any queues (especially in the Summer) it is better to book a table in advance.

# 24. FADO

The streets and alleys of the Portuguese capital were the home of one of our most proud possessions: Fado. Originally sung by sailors and prostitutes in the 18th century, it became associated with the bohemian lives of society's outcasts. Its popularity increased rapidly and soon the low class would sing it anywhere. From the streets to the restaurants and bars' front doors, to prisons, or even while waiting for bullfighting to start. However, it was only in the 20th century that Fado earned its place as part of the Portuguese culture. Amália Rodrigues was the most famous Fado singer in the country and the one who presented it worldwide. In 2011, UNESCO declared it as Intangible Cultural Heritage of Humanity.

Although Fado will always be connected to Lisbon, in Lagos you can also enjoy an evening at a "casa de fados", (fado music house), such as "Alma Lusa" or "Café Vadio" and experience Fado live music with local artists. Since this doesn't happen every night, it is recommended that you book a table in advance.

>TOURIST

# 25. MIDNIGHT BATHING

The 29th of August is always a date to mark on your calendar while visiting Lagos. Dating back to the paganism times before the arrival of Christianity, the locals believed that the devil was on the loose on this day. For this reason, they believed that a bath on sea waters at midnight would cleanse their bodies and souls, almost similar to an atonement. The locals would even say an ocean bath on this day was the equivalent of 29 baths.

To keep this tradition alive, the Lagos municipality hosts the festivities in three different locations: the Cais da Solaria, Praia da Luz and Meia Praia. During the day there are old costume contests, food and drinks and traditional Portuguese folklore music. At night, you will have fireworks and it finishes with an ocean bath at midnight.

The Meia Praia, located east of Lagos, has a privileged view over the city, especially to see the fireworks. If you join the festivities on this location, you will find many groups of young people gathered in circles around fire pits, enjoying their own food and drinks. After midnight, the party goes on with DJs in the restaurants and bars at the beach. Do you believe you can keep up with almost 24h of partying?

Well, in that case, bring warm clothes, and maybe a sleeping bag, and you will be presented with the most beautiful sunrise.

## 26. "PORTUS MAGNUS"

This was the name given by the Romans to the city currently known as Portimão. Much like other areas in the Algarve, there were also found artifacts that prove the existence of human passage from the Neolithic to the Romans, Phoenician, Carthaginian and Moorish. Along with the village of Ferragudo, on the other side of the river Arade, the St. Catharine's Fortress controlled the boats entering the river heading to Silves. For many centuries, the village was an important commercial port and a must-stop for long-haul ships.

The city's industrialization with canned fish factories, in the 19th century, elevated the city of Portimão worldwide with the exportations increasing exponentially. At the time, the city grew and the local authorities provided social housing for the factory workers in nearby neighborhoods. Nowadays, these are the houses of elderly people who used to work at

>TOURIST

those factories. The tall and large brick chimneys you will see in the city are part of the industrial heritage. Since it is considered evidence of industrial archeology, it cannot be demolished and the new construction has to be made around it or be integrated into the new designs.

During the first half of the 20th century, the canned fish industries entered a period of decline, that coincides with the growth of tourism. Nowadays, Portimão is the largest and most populated city in the western Algarve and a reference when it comes to beach tourism.

# 27. THE OLD TOWN

Close to the riverside, there is the oldest part of town, where some of the oldest buildings date back to the Middle Age. One of them is the "Igreja Matriz", where the Christian mass is celebrated. Although it was built in the 15th century, most of its features vanished when the earthquake of 1755 hit the country. Since most of the buildings were demolished or needed to be reconstructed, the church's reconstruction was rushed and many of the original features were modified into the architecture style in use at the time. This is also why you will find only one bell tower, instead of two.

Within a short distance, there is the "Colégio dos Jesuítas", a Christian church built in the 17th century in the Baroque architecture of the time, as well as following the austerity of this religious order. Such as it happened in the rest of the country, the building was severely affected by the earthquake of 1755 and it was rebuilt a few years later. If you enjoy architecture, you will most likely notice different styles in the construction. Over the years, it was refurbished a few times, especially the altar, to preserve the gilded wood carvings.

The city grew around those two buildings and, nowadays, most of the streets accommodate the local and most traditional shops and restaurants. In the "Rua Direita" (straight street, literal translation), you can buy a personalized blend of coffee at "Casa dos Cafés 1940" or some of the best Algarvian wines at "Emporium Romeu". In a short distance, you can also have a taste of the new and modern concepts of canned fished at "Maria do Mar" and, perhaps, take some as a souvenir to your family and friends. And the last, but not the least, the must-stop is "Casa da Isabel". Some of the best Algarvian sweets (traditionally made of almond, carob and orange) can be found here. If you can, please do try all of them, you will not be disappointed. However, if I was forced to name only a few, I would suggest the traditional "Doce Fino" (almond paste filled with Portuguese egg threads) and the "D. Rodrigo" (Portuguese egg threads with sugar syrup and cinnamon). These are my absolute favorite.

# 28. THE RIVERSIDE

Portimão is also known by the Arade's riverside where the locals take a stroll, especially during the morning and at sunset.

Between the railroad and the road bridge, there are some of the best restaurants in town if you are looking for fresh fish. In the Summer, if you don't book a table in advance, probably you will have to wait until there's one available.

After plenty of grilled sardines and an Algarvian white wine, you can enjoy a scenic four-kilometer route along the river, starting on the railroad bridge and walking to Praia da Rocha. Passing through the "Casa Inglesa", a square with a promenade where you can join the locals for an expresso and a "Pastel de Nata", you will get to the Museum of Portimão and the Naval Club, where you can learn how to sail or kayak.

A bit further there are the ruins of an old monastery. Unfortunately, it is private property and is closed for visitors. On your way to Praia da Rocha, you can follow the road or the sidewalk that contours the monastery and takes you closer to the river. From there to the marina, it is a dirt road and the city's commercial port. On your left side, you will have Ferragudo and its castle. If you keep going, you will get to Praia da Rocha's lighthouse and the view is superb.

# 29. SOMETHING OLD, SOMETHING NEW

The Victorian bridal saying can easily be applied to the Museum of Portimão. Located on the Arade's riverbank and within a short distance from the river mouth, the building originally was a canned fish factory. In 2008, the city council bought the property and began the renovation of what is now the museum.

To preserve the industrial heritage, the museum has a permanent exhibition where it showcases the

>TOURIST

complete process of transforming the fresh fish into cans. Due to the richness of the city's history, you can also find Neolithic artifacts, Roman and Moorish daily work tools or 15th century-old cannons recovered from the Arade's riverbed.

# 30. ALCALAR

Within a few kilometers away from Portimão's city center, you can get to know one of the most important Pre-Historic findings in the Algarve. This location includes an ancient necropolis, monoliths and shreds of evidence of an organized settlement.

Since it is an outdoor area, it is only available to be visited during the Summer. The entrance has a small fee that can be bought together or separately from the museum tickets.

# 31. OCEAN REVIVAL

The waters off the coast of Portimão hide a one-of-kind project in the world. The barely known artificial reef, which is one of the largest in Europe, was created by four warships from the Portuguese Navy that were no longer in use. After the ships were stripped of any potentially harmful components that might damage the environment, they were sunken, following a strict protocol to have them in the exact place as it was designed.

Since 2009, when this project began, it has grown and there are still some new elements that are being studied. Nevertheless, the company Subnauta, in Portimão, provides underwater guided tours and the necessary equipment through the circuits designed inside the ships. Also, you will have a unique opportunity to observe many different species of fish, mollusks, anemones and even sea slugs.

>TOURIST

# 32. BEACHES

If you were to ask any Portuguese which is the best beach in Portimão, most of them would say it is Praia da Rocha. And they would be wrong! The sand extends for more than a kilometer, there are plenty of restaurants along the beach and on the cliffs and most of the hotels are within walking distance.

My favorite, however, is Praia do Alemão, also known as Praia do Barranco das Canas (you can find it on InfoPraia app under both names). It is part of Portimão's municipality and only three kilometers away from Praia da Rocha.

Why it is my favorite, you ask? Well… it is much smaller than Praia da Rocha, there aren't any steps to access it, you have plenty of car parking, the bus stops are within walking distance and, most importantly, it is protected from the windy Summer afternoons.

On the east side, on a low tide, you can walk on the sand all the way to Praia da Rocha and visit the Praia do Vau, Praia dos Careanos and Praia dos Três Castelos.

On the west side, there are the cliffs of João d'Arens that you can visit by doing snorkeling, diving or on a paddleboard. As an alternative, you can walk on the cliffs to the nearby beaches of Praia do Submarino, Praia dos Três Irmãos and Prainha. One (very) important piece of advice: due to the erosion there is a high risk of landslides and rockfalls, so it is recommendable that you stay at a safe distance from the edge. Also, avoid wearing flip-flops on this hike. Preferably, wear closed shoes, such as hiking or running shoes.

## 33. I FEEL THE NEED, THE NEED FOR SPEED!

Have you ever felt just like Maverick on Top Gun?

The Autódromo Internacional do Algarve might the answer to your prayers. The only racetrack in the Algarve is considered by many professional drivers and riders as one of the most challenging tracks in the world. In fact, they even nicknamed it the "Rollercoaster", due to the track's design.

In 2020, the Portimão's circuit hosted the Moto GP and the first Formula 1 Portugal Grand Prix in over 25 years.

If you are looking for an afternoon filled with adrenaline, you can select one of the track's racing

>TOURIST

cars and drive on the circuit with the help of a certified instructor. At the Autódromo complex, there are also available motorcycle hot laps and go-karts, some of them suitable for children.

Since the circuit is used all year round by competition teams and component companies for testing, it is recommended that you book these experiences in advance, to guarantee availability.

# 34. THE ANCIENT CAPITAL

Silves is one of the oldest cities in the Algarve. During its most prosperous time, the Romans built bridges, roads and aqueducts that were used later on by the Visigoths and the Moorish. Some of them can be seen even today.

The city itself seems out of a children's fairy tale. Located on top of a hill, Silves grew around its red wall castle and it became one of the most important landmarks in the region. Over the years, archeologists have found artifacts from different times in history, proving that the city is much older than initially thought.

# 35. WHEN A MUSEUM BECOMES THE ARTIFACT

The artifacts found all over the city can be seen in the Silves Municipality Museum of Archeology. It is amazing to observe how many different cultures have inhabited this region!

One curious fact is the museum's central piece. When construction started, the workers found an extremely well-preserved cistern constructed during the Moorish occupation in the 12th century. The construction was stopped immediately and the archaeologists were called in. After all the astonishing details found, the original project was modified and the cistern became the museum's main artifact.

# 36. GET ON THE TIME MACHINE

The Silves Medieval Fair takes place every year, in August, and it will give you a glimpse of the city over the centuries. During one week, Silves transforms itself and you will be taken back in time. It starts with a procession all through the town, presenting the

>TOURIST

warriors, merchants, royals and many other characters that once made Silves their home. Into the night, you will find themed shows from the Castel's to the Cathedral's front door. If you are a foodie, you will find many stands where you can buy typical Portuguese delicacies of Islamic influence.

For you to fully enjoy this experience, head to the Royal Wardrobe and become a royal for the day! The outfits can be rented for a symbolic amount and you can choose anything from a Moorish warrior to a merchant or perhaps a king or simply a peasant.

To make the most out of all the Silves Medieval Fair has to offer, please arrive once the ticket office is open. It usually starts in the late afternoon and the events extend through the night. The later you arrive, the bigger crowds you will find.

# 37. GOING UP THE RIVER

The traditional flat-bottomed boats navigate up the river Arade, between Portimão and Silves, following the same route that the caravels and other larger ships used in the past. The companies providing this experience will let you know all the fun facts and curiosities. Once you get to Silves, you will have around two hours to wander and discover the city by yourself, and then return to the boat.

This experience depends on the tides and, as such, the departure and arrival times may variate. Also, since most of the boats don't provide any shades, better to take a hat and wear sunscreen.

# 38. MONCHIQUE

Over the centuries, ocean travelers reaching the Arade river are amazed by the natural landscape ahead of them. Behind the golden sand beaches lies the foggy hills of the algarvian "Barrocal" (a stretch of land between the coastline and the mountain range), and even further, stands the imponent Monchique mountains.

Scholars who studied the mountain's geological features discovered that the "sienito", a unique type of granite that only exists here, is of volcanic origin. In fact, the warm thermal waters of Caldas de Monchique are evidence of the mountain's volcanic past. In any case, you can rest assured while you visit Monchique. The volcano has long been asleep since

>TOURIST

there are no records of any activity for more than 10.000 years.

Traditionally connected to agriculture and pastoralism, in the last century, the local economy has shifted to tourism, handicraft and traditional foods and drinks.

# 39. THE MOUNTAIN TOP

Fóia is the highest point south of Lisbon, at 902 meters above sea level. From here, on a clear and sunny day, you can see the south coast, Sagres and Cape St. Vincent, the western coast and even a part of Alentejo. The crisp air and the sound of silence are absolutely relaxing!

The locals say it has its own climate, different from anywhere in the mountain. And they are absolutely right! Especially during the Winter, you will see the sky change from clear and sunny to cloudy and foggy in a matter of seconds.

The public trails and roads leading to private properties can be confusing if it is your first visit. For this reason, a jeep safari is a good option if you wish to visit the highest mountain in the Algarve. If you prefer walking, the village website has available a description of several hiking trails.

# 40. THE RAREST WATER IN PORTUGAL

The unique characteristics of the Monchique's waters were recognized by the Romans, who named them "sacred", due to their healing properties. The natural 9,5 alkaline waters were, and still are, used in the treatment of respiratory, urinary and digestive diseases.

Halfway between Portimão and Monchique, there is a secluded valley known as Caldas de Monchique. In the 17th century, the first hotel was built to increase the accommodation available for the many travelers looking to heal their diseases. The popularity of the thermal baths was high and people from all over the country would travel on horseback only to heal their bodies.

Most of the buildings in use today were built in the early 20th century, including some of the hotels and private properties. As such, you will find the charm of old chalets that were once used as summer homes.

>TOURIST

Nowadays, you can visit the location, the hotels, restaurants and bars that were added over the years and, of course, enjoy the spa facilities with treatments specifically designed to use only thermal waters.

# 41. HMMM... YUMMY!

For many years, Monchique was isolated from the rest of the Algarve due to the territory's natural geography and also due to the lack of roads or transportation to the coastal cities. As such, the locals became creative when using what the land provided. Either it was fruits or mushrooms from the woods, the vegetables available on their own garden or the farm animals they raised, everything was availed. Therefore, Monchique's local cuisine is unique in the western Algarve.

The "Enchidos" (smoked or baked sausages) are an ancient method of preserving pork meat over time. Nowadays, they are sold all over the country thanks to their variety and quality.

Another delicacy is the "Bolo do Tacho". The recipe has its origins in the Middle Ages and it was later perfect by the Franciscan friars who lived in the village's convent. Nowadays, it is tradition to have it on the 1st of May, when families reunite in the countryside for a picnic.

The "Bolo do Tacho" is baked on a ceramic pot or pan in a wood oven. The ingredients used are not often combined in a cake recipe, since it is made with cornflour, coffee, cocoa, chocolate, olive oil, lard, salt, honey, cinnamon and sugar. After it is baked, you will have a pudding-like texture on the inside and a darker crust on the outside. The complexity of making this cake is such that I have seen the same recipe being made by three different women at the same time and each cake, although delicious, had a different taste and texture. I know, by the looks of it does not sound that good, but trust me, it is delicious!

The "Tiborna" is another specialty in Monchique. The freshly wood oven-baked bread is eaten still warm and dipped in olive oil and sliced garlic. Its simplicity is sublime and the taste of it is one of my favorites.

I bet you are feeling quite hungry already… well there are a few places where you can try these and other specialties. Restaurants such as "Luar da Fóia", "Jardim das Oliveiras" and "A Charrete" are among some of the oldest and most well-known. If you prefer to taste a bit of all these options, you can try the tapas restaurant "Café Tapas & Wine" or "Tradições".

# 42. THE "MEDRONHO" SPIRIT

The mountain's geography and its climate gather the optimal conditions necessary for the strawberry tree to develop. Although it can be found all over Portugal, Monchique is the place where most of the trees are concentrated.

The strawberry tree fruits have many different applications. Besides being sold at the supermarkets as fresh fruit, it can also be used in juices, jams, cosmetics and pharmaceuticals. The tree is often used as an ornamental piece in gardens.

While you are visiting, if you have the opportunity, try the fruit directly picked from the tree. It will melt in your mouth just like butter. In case you eat too many, you may feel a little buzzed due to the natural alcohol in it.

The most frequent use for the strawberry tree fruit still is the distilled spirit named "Aguardente de Medronho". The translation is not always easy and it is frequently translated to firewater or even moonshine.

The fruit is caught by hand in a mature state and is kept in a closed barrel, away from sunlight. Over the next weeks, the fresh fruit starts to decompose and the natural alcohol is released. When the "mosto", a brownish paste, is prepared, it is taken to the still. Since the knowledge is passed on through generations, usually this process is led by an older man who learned his craft from his father. After a few hours of carefully watching the fire intensity, measuring the alcohol level and the velocity at which the "Aguardente" pours, you will have the opportunity to taste the warm spirit.

How to know you are in the presence of a good glass of "Aguardente"? Well, it is a strong drink, but you should be able to feel the fruit's sweetness along with a warm sensation in your chest.

>TOURIST

# 43. LAGOA

I know, it sounds familiar, right? Although Lagos and Lagoa have very similar names, they are two completely different cities.

Located east of Portimão, Lagoa was named after an old lagoon dried out by the Moorish to extend the agricultural fields.

The land was then filled with orange, almond, carob and olive trees that supplied the whole region. From the hamlets by the sea, came fresh fish and sea salt. The richness of this land attracted humble peasants from all creeds, as well as pirates. The beaches were often raided, which led the people to move further from the sea, into more secure areas. Lagoa flourished as a perfect place to live, halfway between Silves, the kingdom's capital, and the sea.

Nowadays, Lagoa gathers the parishes of Carvoeiro, Ferragudo, Estombar, Parchal and Porches and is known for its wines, standing as the wine capital of the western Algarve.

# 44. THE RIVER MILLS

The hills and valleys along the Arade's riverbank hide a place almost forgotten by time. The first records of Fontes de Estômbar go back to the 15th century when it was documented that a tide mill was built. The farmers along the river took advantage of the river's tide and found a way to grind their own cereals. It was so successful that other mills were built close by.

The Lagoa municipality bought the property in the 1980s and rebuilt one of the mills. Over the years, the property was reconstructed and nowadays it is possible to visit the tide mill, dive in the river waters, enjoy a picnic on the grass or photograph the local birds.

Since 2003, the "Lagoa Jazz Fest" takes place in the Fontes de Estômbar for a week during July. The outdoor amphitheater gains life with musicians from all over the world. The tickets can be purchased online or on-site.

Especially during the Summer, the locals enjoy this place due to its tranquility and calm waters. As such, you may find several families with small children. For you to enjoy it as well, choose the

>TOURIST

weekdays over the weekends to avoid any possible crowd. Also, take your own food and drinks, since there are no restaurants in the area. If you dive, beware that the river bottom is muddy and you might get stuck. Also, the swimming areas are not lifeguarded, so only dive close to the riverbank or if you are a strong swimmer.

Since the Algarve is greatly affected by the Mediterranean climate, the water level may lower during the Summer.

# 45. A HERMITAGE ON THE CLIFFS

Standing on top of the cliff and overlooking the Praia da Nossa Senhora da Rocha, the hermitage of Our Lady of the Rock is one of the greatest mysteries in the western Algarve.

Many scholars have studied the building and are yet to reach an agreement regarding its year of foundation. Some experts believe it is from the 8th century, due to the existence of a Visigothic chapiter, and others believe it was constructed much later in the 15th century, by the Portuguese Christians. Due to the lack of archeological findings and excavations, it is difficult to know for sure. Some documents suggest that the hermitage was part of a fortress built to protect the beach and a small port from the frequent pirate raids.

Nowadays, only the hermitage is left standing with its pristine white walls and it is one of the most important landmarks in Lagoa's municipality. And the view… it is breath-taking!

# 46. A FISHERMEN'S VILLAGE

Carvoeiro is a unique fishing village. Since the Romans, the beach has always been the central element and, over time, the housing and population grew around it. The beach provided easy access to the ocean and the cliffs provided the necessary protection from windy storms. With such perfect conditions, fishing quickly became the most important activity for the local economy. Similar to what happened in other villages and cities in the Algarve, in the 1960s, Carvoeiro observed a change from fishing activities to tourism.

Within walking distance, you can visit the unmatched cliff formation of Algar Seco and choose

>TOURIST

to enjoy the ocean view from the top or walk down the stair and get closer to the water. The best part is "A Boneca" (the doll, as the local fisherman named it). While you are on land, it will seem as if you were standing on a balcony carved on the cliff and if you see it from the sea, it looks like the eyes of a doll.

# 47. THE WESTERN ALGARVE WONDERS

I'm sure you are curious as to why I would use such a confident title. There is simply no other way to describe the beaches I am about to tell you.

The "Praia da Marinha" was enlisted as one of the most beautiful in the world by the Michelin Guide, the European Best Destinations and (twice) by the North-American news broadcaster CNN. The natural arches sculpted on the cliffs by the waves are the must-see, however, you can also enjoy a light meal at the beach restaurant or an afternoon of sunbathing.

Close by there is another natural wonder that you would not want to miss: The Benagil Cave. Located by the village and beach with the same name, this cave is one of the biggest of its kind. The main feature is the natural dome shape breached by the sunlight coming from a hole in the ceiling. This cave is so big, it has its own private beach! Since it is very close to the Praia de Benagil, the visitors might be tempted to swim to the cave. For your own safety, get on a guided tour. This is a place of frequent and swift tide and current changes and even if you are a strong swimmer, you might easily get trapped inside the cave.

The Praia do Carvalho is lesser known than the former two, but its history is much more fascinating. Such as other beaches all over the Algarve, originally this was only accessible by boat and was too far for the local fishermen to make any use of it. For this reason, raiders and pirates found it to be the perfect place for smuggling. A path was carved by hand inside the cliff, which is used even today as the only walking access to the beach. If you are facing the ocean and look to your right-hand side, you will notice another path carved onto the cliff's side. This was used by smugglers to get merchandise into the larger boats that could not get closer to the shore.

If you visit Praia do Carvalho you will find a steep and narrow path to reach the beach, not advisable for people with walking disabilities. From my personal experience, I strongly advise you to wear hiking shoes or some other that adheres to the floor. Shoes

>TOURIST

such as flip-flops or sandals may slip and put you at risk of falling.

# 48. HOME IS WHERE YOUR HEARTH IS

And my heart is in my hometown. Welcome to Ferragudo!

The locals have named it the Algarve's Venice since, in older times, the river Arade would flow into the village and the only mean of transportation would be the boat. Due to the infrastructures built in the village, nowadays this is a rare sight.

Excavations and archeological artifacts found all over the village trace its origins to the Neolithic times. The Phoenicians and the Carthaginians have also left some belongings as proof of their passage and the Romans and Moorish occupied the village for a long time before the Christians arrived. From its early existence, Ferragudo was an important fishing and commercial port.

The 16$^{th}$ century marked the village's recognition of its strategic location and importance to the local economy. The Fort of São João do Arade's construction served a doubled purpose: to protect the people and control the river's mouth. At the time, the shores were constantly raided by pirates who pillaged everything on their path. Some of them, including Vikings, tried to reach Silves and its castle. Along with the Saint Catherine's Fortress on the Portimão riverbank, the fort would help secure access to the capital of the Algarve kingdom.

After the construction of the Fort of São João do Arade, the population felt secure enough to live in the vicinity and the number of people living in Ferragudo grew over the years.

Similar to what happened to other coastal cities and villages, Ferragudo was filled with canned fish industries in the early 20th century. Today, the industries are gone and tourism has assumed the central place in the local economy.

## 49. THE "AZULEJOS"

The traditional Portuguese tiles are an expression of our culture and heritage. This form of art has its origins during the Moorish occupation in the Iberian Peninsula. At the time, the Islamic artisans passed on their craft to the local artists who, over the years,

>TOURIST

created a unique style. With the Portuguese Discoveries, the "azulejos" traveled around the world and can now be seen in several monuments as ornamental pieces, both in and outside of the buildings.

As a way to celebrate this part of our history, Ferragudo's narrow streets are filled with tile pieces made by local artisans, depicting the village's history.

So, how great would be to have your own "azulejo" made? At the atelier "Arti Arte Azulejar", besides enjoying and purchasing the local artwork, you can be part of a workshop and learn all there is to know about this craft. The workshops are available for short periods, so it is recommended that you book in advance.

# 50. DISCOVERING FERRAGUDO

To complete your journey through the Western Algarve, I took the liberty of planning your last day.

Start the day at "Quente Quentinho" with freshly baked bread with melted butter, a "Pastel de Nata" and an expresso. As an alternative, they also have available an English breakfast menu. While you are sitting, take a look around. You will see the tile artwork almost everywhere, from your plates to the house's exterior walls.

Once you finish, walk along the river canal towards the west. You will find the village's main square on your left. All festivities, such as the village's 500 years old take place here. Also, during the Summer, local artists play on a stage assembled at its center and people gather on the restaurant's promenades to enjoy the warm nights.

Following the same path, on your right-hand side, you will find the Arade river overflowing with fishermen boats carrying seagulls, cormorants and terns that feed on these calm waters. On the river's wall, the local fishermen gather their nets and the handmade octopus traps to prepare the boats and nets for the next fishing trip.

The next street you see on your left will take you wandering through narrow streets and white-washed houses. Each front door has a unique décor composed of flower vases and pink ivy blossoms.

Once you reach the church, you will be amazed by the view. The Church of Our Lady of Conception was built on the village's highest point as it was intended to bless and overwatch the fishing boat's departure. Nowadays, you can enjoy a relaxing view over the Arade river.

>TOURIST

Since you are so close to the sea, you must try the freshest fish in the village. The restaurant "Sueste" and its promenade overlooking the river will welcome you for one of the best meals you will ever have. The waiter will advise you and, depending on what fish you choose, will let know if it is better to have it grilled or boiled.

Beside the restaurant, there is the tiniest street squeezed between the houses. This will lead you to Praia da Angrinha, a beach where the river meets the ocean. On the horizon, there is the Fort of São João do Arade. In case the tide is low, you will be able to walk along the water and pass just below the fort. Just after you passed it, you are at Praia Grande. This is the longest beach in Ferragudo parish and the one preferred by families with small children due to the calm waters.

From now on, I will lead you through a pathway only known by a few. On the other end of Praia Grande, there are some cliffs. If you enjoy swimming with fewer people, this is a great place. However, this is not the final destination. The path along the cliffs will take you over to the nearby beaches, only accessible by boats, and further on you will find Praia do Molhe, where the pier separates the ocean from the river and protects the river mouth. Leading on, the next beach is Praia do Pintadinho. The easy access to this beach and its shallow waters makes it one of the most frequented.

And now, on to my favorite place in Ferragudo. Continuing over the cliffs, you will get to a lighthouse named Ponta do Altar. In ancient times, there was an altar that unfortunately vanished due to sea erosion. This place is also a reference for marine archeologists, since in 1992, eight bronze cannons were found in the vicinity, along with several other smaller artifacts that are thought to belong to a Portuguese or Spanish ship from the 17th century.

However, what makes this my favorite place is the landscape. On a clear day, you can see Sagres promontory (more than 40 kilometers away), Ponta da Piedade, Lagos, Praia da Rocha, Portimão and the river Arade with the Monchique mountains in sight.

I wish that you enjoy it as much as I do and I look forward to welcoming you!

>TOURIST

# TOP REASONS TO BOOK THIS TRIP

**Landscape**: The Western Algarve has a rich and unique landscape.

**History**: Meet our past and understand our present.

**Food**: The Mediterranean cuisine at its best.

# PACKING AND PLANNING TIPS

### A Week before Leaving

- Arrange for someone to take care of pets and water plants.

- Email and Print important Documents.

- Get Visa and vaccines if needed.

- Check for travel warnings.

- Stop mail and newspaper.

- Notify Credit Card companies where you are going.

- Passports and photo identification is up to date.

- Pay bills.

- Copy important items and download travel Apps.

- Start collecting small bills for tips.

- Have post office hold mail while you are away.

- Check weather for the week.

- Car inspected, oil is changed, and tires have the correct pressure.

- Check airline luggage restrictions.

- Download Apps needed for your trip.

# >TOURIST

## Right Before Leaving

- Contact bank and credit cards to tell them your location.

- Clean out refrigerator.

- Empty garbage cans.

- Lock windows.

- Make sure you have the proper identification with you.

- Bring cash for tips.

- Remember travel documents.

- Lock door behind you.

- Remember wallet.

- Unplug items in house and pack chargers.

- Change your thermostat settings.

- Charge electronics, and prepare camera memory cards.

# READ OTHER
# GREATER THAN A TOURIST
# BOOKS

*Greater Than a Tourist- California: 50 Travel Tips from Locals*

*Greater Than a Tourist- Salem Massachusetts USA50 Travel Tips from a Local by Danielle Lasher*

*Greater Than a Tourist United States: 50 Travel Tips from Locals*

*Greater Than a Tourist- St. Croix US Birgin Islands USA: 50 Travel Tips from a Local by Tracy Birdsall*

*Greater Than a Tourist- Montana: 50 Travel Tips from a Local by Laurie White*

*Children's Book: Charlie the Cavalier Travels the World by Lisa Rusczyk Ed. D.*

# > TOURIST

Follow us on Instagram for beautiful travel images:
http://Instagram.com/GreaterThanATourist

Follow *Greater Than a Tourist* on Amazon.

CZYKPublishing.com

# > TOURIST

At *Greater Than a Tourist*, we love to share travel tips with you. How did we do? What guidance do you have for how we can give you better advice for your next trip? Please send your feedback to GreaterThanaTourist@gmail.com as we continue to improve the series. We appreciate your constructive feedback. Thank you.

>TOURIST

# METRIC CONVERSIONS

## TEMPERATURE

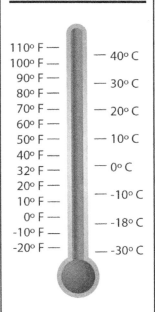

110° F — — 40° C
100° F —
90° F — — 30° C
80° F —
70° F — — 20° C
60° F —
50° F — — 10° C
40° F —
32° F — — 0° C
20° F —
10° F — — -10° C
0° F — — -18° C
-10° F —
-20° F — — -30° C

### To convert F to C:
Subtract 32, and then multiply by 5/9 or .5555.

### To Convert C to F:
Multiply by 1.8 and then add 32.

### 32F = 0C

## LIQUID VOLUME

*To Convert:.....................Multiply by*
*U.S. Gallons to Liters............... 3.8*
*U.S. Liters to Gallons .................26*
*Imperial Gallons to U.S. Gallons 1.2*
*Imperial Gallons to Liters....... 4.55*
*Liters to Imperial Gallons ........22*
**1 Liter = .26 U.S. Gallon**
**1 U.S. Gallon = 3.8 Liters**

## DISTANCE

*To convert ..............Multiply by*
*Inches to Centimeters ....2.54*
*Centimeters to Inches ........39*
*Feet to Meters......................... .3*
*Meters to Feet ....................3.28*
*Yards to Meters ...................91*
*Meters to Yards ................1.09*
*Miles to Kilometers ..........1.61*
*Kilometers to Miles............ .62*
**1 Mile = 1.6 km**
**1 km = .62 Miles**

## WEIGHT

1 Ounce  =  .28 Grams
1 Pound  =  .4555 Kilograms
1 Gram  =  .04 Ounce
1 Kilogram  =  2.2 Pounds

85

# TRAVEL QUESTIONS

- Do you bring presents home to family or friends after a vacation?

- Do you get motion sick?

- Do you have a favorite billboard?

- Do you know what to do if there is a flat tire?

- Do you like a sun roof open?

- Do you like to eat in the car?

- Do you like to wear sun glasses in the car?

- Do you like toppings on your ice cream?

- Do you use public bathrooms?

- Did you bring a cell phone and does it have power?

- Do you have a form of identification with you?

- Have you ever been pulled over by a cop?

- Have you ever given money to a stranger on a road trip?

- Have you ever taken a road trip with animals?

- Have you ever gone on a vacation alone?

- Have you ever run out of gas?

## >TOURIST

- If you could move to any place in the world, where would it be?

- If you could travel anywhere in the world, where would you travel?

- If you could travel in any vehicle, which one would it be?

- If you had three things to wish for from a magic genie, what would they be?

- If you have a driver's license, how many times did it take you to pass the test?

- What are you the most afraid of on vacation?

- What do you want to get away from the most when you are on vacation?

- What foods smell bad to you?

- What item do you bring on ever trip with you away from home?

- What makes you sleepy?

- What song would you love to hear on the radio when you're cruising on the highway?

- What travel job would you want the least?

- What will you miss most while you are away from home?

- What is something you always wanted to try?

- What is the best road side attraction that you ever saw?

- What is the farthest distance you ever biked?

- What is the farthest distance you ever walked?

- What is the weirdest thing you needed to buy while on vacation?

- What is your favorite candy?

- What is your favorite color car?

- What is your favorite family vacation?

- What is your favorite food?

- What is your favorite gas station drink or food?

- What is your favorite license plate design?

- What is your favorite restaurant?

- What is your favorite smell?

- What is your favorite song?

- What is your favorite sound that nature makes?

- What is your favorite thing to bring home from a vacation?

- What is your favorite vacation with friends?

- What is your favorite way to relax?

- Where is the farthest place you ever traveled in a car?

## >TOURIST

- Where is the farthest place you ever went North, South, East and West?

- Where is your favorite place in the world?

- Who is your favorite singer?

- Who taught you how to drive?

- Who will you miss the most while you are away?

- Who if the first person you will contact when you get to your destination?

- Who brought you on your first vacation?

- Who likes to travel the most in your life?

- Would you rather be hot or cold?

- Would you rather drive above, below, or at the speed limited?

- Would you rather drive on a highway or a back road?

- Would you rather go on a train or a boat?

- Would you rather go to the beach or the woods?

# TRAVEL BUCKET LIST

1.

2.

3.

4.

5.

6.

7.

8.

9.

10.

Printed in Great Britain
by Amazon